WORKBOOK
FOR

ADULT CHILDREN OF EMOTIONALLY IMMATURE PARENTS

HOW TO HEAL FROM DISTANT, REJECTING,

OR SELF-INVOLVED PARENTS

By

LINDSAY C. GIBSON

Proudly Brought To You By

WRIGHT PUBLISHERS

Table of Contents

HOW TO USE THIS WORKBOOK

This book is to be used to raise awareness or shine a light on your past so you can recover from childhood emotional loneliness and injuries.

As you attempt the questions and go through the book, you may notice that you experience intense emotional sensations. This is normal, as hidden pain is coming to the fore. When you get over it (as many times as it surfaces) you'll find out that you're calm from within.

Take your time to go through the various parts of each chapter. No section or subdivision is a mistake or an afterthought. I advise that you digest them all and not skip any part.

P.S. Just because the intense emotions have lifted the first time, it doesn't mean you're free forever. I'll advise that you revisit this workbook as many times as possible. You're dealing with pain and issues that have been happening for many years; it's utterly impossible for it to disappear at once.

INTRODUCTION

Adult Children of Emotionally Immature Parents by Lindsay C. Gibson, PsyD is a book to help raise awareness about the effect of emotionally immature parents on the lives of their children. Without the awareness that there's a problem, it is impossible to seek a solution.

Many lives have been damaged indelibly as a result of emotionally immature parents but with this book, you'll find out there's hope for you. Everyone who wants to be free from toxic parents must emotionally disengage from them. This is why understanding who you're dealing with is the most important thing.

With this book, you'll be able to fill the emotional gaps that exist in your life. You'll see that your past or your parents (as the case may be) are the hindrances to your ability to love and live the life you've always craved.

With this book, you'll gain an understanding of yourself and your loved ones. You'll break free from all inhibitions you grew up with. You can live your life first for yourself, and allow yourself to think freely rather than fall back to outdated family patterns.

Who should use this workbook

There's no restriction when it comes to who can use this book. If you've experienced emotional loneliness as a child or adult, if you've ever felt a separateness or distance between you and everyone, if you feel like no one understands you and no one ever will, if you've learned to listen to the inner critic voice and you obey it without reluctance, then you need the book.

Everyone who grew up with emotionally immature parents or caregivers also needs this book.

The truth is, we all have injuries from childhood that we need to heal and be free from. As long as you do, then you can use this book.

What is in the book and why is it important?

As the name suggests, *Adult Children of Emotionally Immature Parents* focuses on how to heal from distant, rejecting, or self-involved parents.

This book is important because it offers a different approach to how to be free from childhood emotional neglect and injuries caused by emotionally immature parents.

There's something enticing about staying with the familiar. It's the reason a child of an abusive parent will end up with an abusive partner or abuse their partners. By reading this book, you can correct old patterns that will make you continue the emotionally immature cycle.

This book offers you the opportunity of true freedom as you live the life you're meant to live with no holding back, no fear, no worry or concern about your parents or anyone who hurt you. The past is understood and the future is new and free.

CHAPTER 1: HOW EMOTIONALLY IMMATURE PARENTS AFFECT THEIR ADULT CHILDREN'S LIVES

Summary

We are born with an emotional bank and when there are no deposits made, we experience emotional loneliness. This can begin from childhood and linger on to adulthood.

The pain you feel as a result of being invincible by others, especially those you love is as tangible as physical pain. The only difference is that it doesn't show physically.

Signs of emotional loneliness are gut feelings of emptiness, feeling no one can understand you, and being alone. This is what happens when you didn't gain enough empathy from others, especially your caregivers.

Emotional intimacy is important. It entails having someone you can share your life, your burdens, and feelings with. You can be vulnerable and feel safe with this person.

In a relationship, there must be mutual emotional responsiveness. Without it, a relationship can't thrive.

Many people lack self-confidence due to parental rejection. They are emotionally neglected as children and expect the same from others. They don't have the confidence that anyone will take note of them.

Key takeaways from this chapter

- There are parents who look perfect, they have everything you want and you may secretly wish that you're them or they are your parents; however, they may be emotionally immature. Looks can be deceiving.
- Emotional loneliness is felt deep within and it can't be seen which is why it can be easily overlooked.
- Without self-awareness, you may not understand what the emotional deficit is and how to get the desired change you need.
- Children who experience emotional loneliness put people's needs before their own, they do everything to show they don't really have emotional needs and this prevents them from making proper emotional connections. They are quick to become self-sufficient and they grow up quickly.
- The answer to a lack of emotional loneliness is an attentive and reliable emotional relationship.

Lessons

- If you grow up with parents who are emotionally immature, you'll experience loneliness.
- Children who grow up with emotionally immature parents experience core emptiness as they grow up. The emptiness within remains even if they have everything they want in life.
- People who are emotionally deprived as children end up in the same kind of relationship or marriage as grown-ups. This is because it's comforting to stay within the familiar.

- Parents who are emotionally immature don't know how to approve the feelings of their children. This makes children give in to whatever others are certain about.

Goals

- To be emotionally mature
- To learn emotional intimacy

Action plan

- Understanding emotional maturity
- To properly describe emotional immaturity and loneliness
- Understanding the importance of emotional intimacy
- To learn how to listen to your emotions
- To know the signs of emotional loneliness in children

Questions

1. Can you describe your earliest feeling of emotional loneliness?
2. What's the remedy for emotional loneliness for a child who has an emotionally mature parent?
3. How can you distinguish between a child who grew up with emotionally mature parents and one who didn't?
4. What are the signs to identify an emotionally immature parent?
5. How does emotional intimacy sustain relationships?

CHAPTER 2: RECOGNIZING THE EMOTIONALLY IMMATURE PARENT

Summary

It's difficult to look at your parents objectively because your relationship with them is subjective so it may feel like betrayal. However, you need to be able to do this so you can understand the reasons behind their limitations.

Anyone who is emotionally immature reacts impulsively. They don't think about how their attitude affects others. They see nothing wrong in what they do and see no reason to apologize to others. They also never experience regret.

Many emotionally immature people didn't have an emotionally intimate or supportive connection with their own parents when they were children. They decided to toughen up to get through their own emotional loneliness.

Many emotionally immature people fear their feelings and find deep and conflicting emotions threatening. They pass on their fear of vulnerability to their children.

Emotionally immature people usually grow up in a family that restrained their emotions and intellect. This is why they grow up having an oversimplified outlook on life and rigid coping mechanism.

Key takeaways from this chapter

Parents who are emotionally immature can impact their children negatively, especially in areas of relationship, self-confidence, and self-esteem. This leads to excessive caution in their love lives and relationship with others.

Characteristics of emotionally mature people

When a person is emotionally mature,

- They can think objectively and conceptually while connecting with the other person emotionally.
- They know what they want and they get it without taking advantage of other people.
- They are comfortable with their emotions and feelings.
- They are great with their relationships with other people and they get involved in other people's lives.
- They can be vulnerable and intimate
- They are great with conflict resolution
- They don't react impulsively and they are emotionally intelligent.
- They know how to handle stress properly and they process their thoughts and feelings without living in denial
- They have a grip on their emotions and reality. They relate with others with empathy and humor while improving their relationship with others.

When a person is emotionally immature,

- They aren't flexible in their thoughts and their decisions. They are impulsive and narrow-minded, focusing on one thing they can do and closing their minds to all other things.
- They don't cope well under stress. They come up with coping mechanisms to help deny, distort and change their reality.
- They find it difficult to calm down when they are upset
- They play the blame game and find solace in substances, medication, and intoxicants
- They think only within their framework and do what they think is best according to their feelings at the moment.
- They are subjective and how they feel is more important than everything else.
- They don't understand or respect other people's differences and opinions. They would rather stay with people with like minds.
- They act childishly. Even though they are, they wouldn't see themselves as insecure or defensive.
- They are always self-involved and self-preoccupied due to anxiety during childhood and they are filled with doubts.
- They are the reference for themselves. They always make themselves the center of attention.
- They are into role reversal. They treat their children as parents, expecting the children to pay attention to them.
- They have little or no empathy and they lack any form of emotional sensitivity.

Effects of being emotionally shut down

- They grew up too early with little or no acceptance
- They were built to fit for their families
- They are rigid and unable to develop fluidly
- They are difficult to understand and inconsistent
- They have a strong defense system which has become a core part of who they are
- They shut down or deny their emotions to focus on the physical. They are ignorant of their children's emotional needs.
- They are killjoys because they can't show genuine emotions due to fear.
- They have strong but shallow emotions.

Lessons

- You need to understand your parents' superficial behavioral characteristics as well as their emotional framework. This will help you understand them better, you'll know how to describe and categorize their behaviors and nothing they do to you will catch you unawares.
- It's important to know what it means to be emotionally mature.
- Many parents who are emotionally immature had to shut down some of their feelings so their parents could also accept them. This made it difficult or impossible for them to explore, understand, express their feelings and also develop their unique identity.

Goals

- Identifying emotionally maturity
- Identifying people and the traits of people who are emotionally mature
- To view your parents objectively

Action plan

- To grow out of emotional immaturity
- To become emotionally mature
- To outgrow emotional immaturity as parents

Questions

1. What are some of the things that led to many emotionally immature parents?
2. Is it possible for emotionally immature parents to ever change? If your answer is yes, what can they do? If your answer is no, why not?
3. How does growing up in an emotionally immature family affect an individual's outlook on life?
4. Do you recognize areas in your life that show you're emotionally immature? Can you mention them and how it affects you?

CHAPTER 3: HOW IT FEELS TO HAVE A RELATIONSHIP WITH AN EMOTIONALLY IMMATURE PARENT

Summary

Since we share bonds with our parents, it's more painful and disappointing to grow up with emotionally immature parents.

Emotionally immature parents have a challenge when it comes to accountability and consequences for their actions whether in the past or in the future.

Emotionally immature people don't have a resolute sense of self. They also have the wrong impression of family closeness or intimacy. They lack the ability for real communication because they lack empathy and they sulk at building bridges or mending relationships. They don't know how to be sensitive to other people.

They focus on the impression that others create about them and they defend that their anxiety trumps others no matter who it is.

Key takeaways from this chapter

Our first attachment is to our parents and members of our families. Even if we reach out to others for different things, we still turn back to our parents to bond with them.

The easiest way to identify emotional immaturity is in relationships. The consequences can be devastating when it happens within a parent-child relationship.

Communication is near impossible if you grew up with emotionally immature parents. This means communication is usually one-sided and only one person draws all the attention.

Some children of emotionally immature parents don't vent their anger. They can repress it or turn it against themselves or deny it. They act out their emotional needs instead of speaking up about it. They do nothing to understand the emotional needs of others even if others might mean their children.

It's a pain to live with emotionally immature people because they have poor receptive capacity; they want you to proffer solutions yet they don't accept helpful solutions.

Emotionally immature people:

- Expect that you read their minds and understand what they are going through.
- Expect everyone including their children to mirror them.
- Only feel good when everyone bows to their needs.
- They see life in black and white, which means they bring everything to either good or bad. They get defensive if you point out anything they did wrong.

- Believe everyone should stick to their roles yet they don't how to respect boundaries especially when it comes to their children. This can involve guilt-tripping or shaming their kids.
- Can have a fragmented orientation of time when they get emotional. They are governed by how they feel at the moment and they don't learn from their past mistakes, nor do they anticipate the future.
- Seem like emotional manipulators because they are opportunistic especially when it comes to doing things in their favor.
- Their emotions, stress, and anxiety make them act like children all over again.

Emotional intimacy and enmeshment are the same to them. They have favorites which isn't a show of any special affection but it may be that the other child or children weren't dependent on them enough.

Lessons

- Just as we don't have a say in the families we are born into, so it is with the earliest relationship in our life.
- Sometimes anger and rage are coping mechanisms for feelings of abandonment. This is the energy that serves as a boost to enable individuals protests against feelings or emotions they don't like.
- Emotional contagion is akin to tantrums in babies and young children as this is their method of voicing out their displeasure or needs. They act in ways that make everyone uncomfortable until everyone makes sure they are satisfied.

- Emotionally immature individuals don't always recognize that they are in need of emotional comfort since they are oblivious to their own emotional needs.

  Emotionally mature people show empathy and are self-aware which makes it difficult to overlook other people's feelings.
- There's a difference between enmeshment and emotional intimacy. Enmeshment can either be seen as idealization or dependency. Emotionally immature parents can act out enmeshment with other people to fill their void.

Goals

- To understand what it means to have a relationship with an emotionally immature parent.
- To become aware of the signs of growing up with emotionally immature parents.
- To know what emotionally mature parents do.

Action plans

- Identifying if you grew up with emotionally immature parents.
- Knowing the signs and consequences of growing up with emotionally immature parents.
- Doing what emotionally mature parents do

Questions

1. Why is it more devasting when a child has an emotionally immature parent?

2. As a child, what did your parents do that hurt you the most? Did they fail to give you any attention, were they insensitive to your feelings, did they constantly shut you up, were they too strict, were you not the favorite child, did they continually shame you? Mention them.

3. Have you ever repressed your anger or used it against yourself? What happened?

4. Following up with the previous question, if your daughter felt that way, what would you say to her, and how would you help her?

5. Can you describe an action you witnessed between an emotionally immature parent and their child?

6. Is emotional labor hard work? Explain the reason for your answer.

Chapter 4: FOUR TYPES OF EMOTIONALLY IMMATURE PARENTS

Summary

There are four types of emotionally immature parents: emotional parents, driven parents, passive parents, and rejecting parents.

All four of them are self-absorbed and self-involved, so they don't know how to be emotionally available to their children. They all lack empathy so it's difficult to relate with them. They make others feel drained.

All four of them are scared of showing their true feelings and they seek their comfort by controlling other people.

They aren't emotionally available and their children feel emotionally invincible.

They sulk at interpersonal relationships.

Key takeaways from this chapter

- The four types of emotionally immature parents are narcissistic, self-absorbed, and emotionally unreliable.

Emotionally immature parents:

- Use their children to make themselves feel better, thereby overwhelming their children with adult issues.
- Can't see their different children as separate individuals but see them based on their own needs as a parent.

- Have children who are de-selfed because their needs are swallowed up by the needs of their parents.

The emotional parents

- Emotional parents display extreme emotions which can be over-involvement at one extreme and abrupt withdrawal at another extreme. This tells you how unstable they are, how riddled they are with anxiety, and how little things can tip them off.
- To them, everyone can either be classified as a rescuer or an abandoner.
- They are childish and they let everyone feel they are fragile.
- When they are experiencing a bad time, they take their children with them so they feel their anger, pain, rage, and emotional meltdown. As a result of this, children with such parents grow up to yield to other people's wishes even to their own detriment.
- The only thing they can be sure about their parents is their emotional instability (which perhaps is their biggest issue); even though they may not easily agree to it, their parents are mentally ill.
- They have blunt attacks that can drive others to suicidal thoughts or attempts. They make people nervous as no one knows what to expect from them.
- They can't handle stress and they are emotionally imbalanced. They are susceptible to substance addiction. This is why they are unreliable, impulsive, and intimidating although, this may not be

obvious when they are outside their home or in a structured setting.

- They see the world in black and white, they keep a record of wrongs done to them with the intention of reciprocating.

The driven parent

- Driven parents are perfectionists, they are super busy and goal-oriented. They hardly take a break and when they do, it's not long enough for them to see the emotional needs of their children. However, they always have a say when it comes to running other people's lives.

- Their sense of perfection makes them run the lives of their children even when they are adults. They fear the child might not get things right.

- They appear to be normal but they aren't which makes it difficult for anyone to comprehend their egocentrism.

- They make sure they invest all into the success of their child. Even if the weight of what they are doing is crushing the child, they are oblivious to it. They make their children feel like they scrutinize and evaluate them constantly.

- Children of driven parents have a hard time taking the initiative and they are usually unmotivated and depressed.

- They easily make assumptions about others while keeping the focus on themselves. They pretend to have everything under control.

- They drive their children to a career they feel is the best for them while focusing on the traits they love n the child and staying blind to other traits.

- A strong fear for them is their children becoming unsuccessful and that drives them. It's more important to meet goals than to understand their children. They are self-made and proud of it.

The passive parent

- Passive parents are passive. They avoid anything that can upset them, they are happy to take the back seat and their coping mechanisms involve acquiescing and minimizing problems.

- They easily flow with people who have dominant personalities

- Even though they seem more emotionally available, they are detached and passive, and they withdraw. Like ostriches, they hide their head in the sand when anything is displeasing around them.

- They are immature but since they are playful it conceals this trait. They can be the most playful parent and they show empathy more than other types. However, they do this only because the needs of others don't get in their way.

- They can leverage a child's openness to them and use it for their own good. The child who enjoys being open to them would find out that their relationship is somewhat unhealthy while risking the displeasure of the other parent who may feel jealous.

- Children of passive parents grow up to make excuses for the abandoning behavior of others.

The rejecting parent

- Rejecting parents act like they don't need and deserve a family. They choose to be unbothered by their children, they give out commands and live in their own world.
- They enclose themselves and shut everyone even their children out. The children feel it would be better if they didn't exist.
- Such parents are quite touchy and irritable so their children know it's best to stay out of their way. If their children should push them to evoke an emotional reaction, they may only receive an angry or abusive response.
- Everything revolves around them and everyone around them leaves to give them what they want.
- Children of such parents are quick to assume they bother others and as much as they can, they avoid making requests and try to get what they need by themselves without involving anyone.

Lessons

- Growing up with emotionally immature parents can lead to loneliness and insecurity.
- The level of empathy and sensitivity displayed by mothers has a strong influence on the baby's attachment behaviors between a mother and her child.

Goals

- To know the four types of emotionally immature parents

- To know the distinct traits of the different types of emotionally immature parents

Action plans

- Knowing the four types of emotionally immature parents
- Knowing their distinct characteristics
- Knowing what to look out for when you come across any of them

Questions

1. What are the four types of emotionally mature parents?
2. Mention ten characteristics of each of the four types.
3. Using your experiences, describe the kind of parents you had while growing up with any of these traits.
4. Is it possible to have an emotionally balanced parent? Can you be one? What can you do better?

CHAPTER 5: HOW DIFFERENT CHILDREN REACT TO EMOTIONALLY IMMATURE PARENTING

Summary

Children have their own way of reacting to their parents' emotional immaturity. They come up with subconscious healing fantasies on how things would improve.

If children know that their true self isn't accepted, they will develop a role-self in order to retain their position as a valuable part of the family.

Healing fantasies give children optimism that they will have a bright future.

When children have emotionally immature parents, they develop either of two major skills: externalizing or internalizing. Externalizers believe the solution is without while internalizers believe the answers are within. This means internalizers are prone to inner distress.

Key takeaways from this chapter

- Coping strategies make the true child hide themselves in the family.
- All emotionally deprived children come up with a healing fantasy to make life be what it's meant to be for them.
- It takes successful marital therapy to help people see that they are trying to force their partners to get that sweet childhood they were deprived of.

- Stepping into a role-self isn't deliberate. It is something created via what you see, trials and errors, and what you wish you had. It can either be positive or negative.
- Parents can influence role-selves in children.
- Role-selves derive their energy and vitality from the true self. There is a limit to which you can play a role as you can't do it all your life. You need to constantly recharge it because your role-self doesn't want to be revealed as an imposter.
- Children who are internalizers think they have the ability to change things on their own but externalizers expect others to bring solutions.
- Internalizers can become externalizers when they are under undue pressure and stress. They can turn to affairs to take away the pressure even though the guilt and shame may push them further into it.

Internalizers

- They have a lot going on in their mind, they take deep reflections and they always want to learn from past mistakes
- They are sensitive and pay attention to cause and effect
- They believe that by developing themselves and with more hard work they become better.
- They take responsibility for their actions.
- The source of their anxiety is the guilt that comes from displeasing others.
- They over-sacrifice and later resent what they do for others.

- They blame themselves excessively so this elicits support from others.
- They suffer in silence and they look great even if they are dying on the inside

Externalizers

- They are impulsive and reactive; they take action before thinking. They don't reflect on what they do and they pass the blame to others rather than take their share of the blame.
- Life is trial and error and they don't learn from their mistakes.
- They believe that things need to change on the outside for them to be happy within.
- They believe those who are competent are meant to help them
- They have poor self-confidence and superior complex.
- They depend on external soothing which is why they are prone to substance abuse, addictions, and addictive relationships.
- Their anxiety is caused by being cut off from external sources of security.
- They are attracted to impulsive people and they depend on others for their security and support.
- They throw tantrums until they get help from others
- Their actions usually lead to punishment and rejection and they live out their pain, depression, and anxiety.
- Their use of denial makes them avoid shame and make the right changes. It leads them to impulsiveness and overwhelming failure which leads to more impulsiveness.

- They can be abusive siblings, they can incite emotional abuse by driving everyone with their troubles and tantrums.

Lessons

To find what they aren't receiving from their parents, children of emotionally immature parents create a self-role which is what to do to get the attention of their parents.

No coping strategy will ever allow a child to become who they are truly meant to be. This is because the child becomes whoever they need in order to cope.

Healing fantasies affect adult relationships because it makes individuals secretly expect that their closest relationships will bring the desired healing.

People are usually oblivious to the fact that they are imposing their unrealistic healing fantasies on others. Only outsiders who don't have this fantasy know that it is unrealistic.

Children who grew up with emotionally immature parents manage emotional deficiency in two ways; it can be either by internalizing their problems or externalizing them. A child can be an internalist or externalist but will adopt the one coping style to meet a certain need.

Externalists rarely grow psychologically while internalists can grow psychologically due to self-reflection.

Emotionally immature parents are quick to help out externalizing children to make life easier for them since the externalizing child makes impulsive choices that can affect all.

People who opt for therapy and read about self-help would have an internalizing coping mechanism.

Goals

- To identify your childhood fantasy
- To identify your role-self
- To identify what led to your role self
- To identify the effects of role-self
- To identify your healing fantasy

Action plan

- Outgrowing your childhood fantasy
- Identifying your role-self
- Identifying and dealing with your role self
- Identifying your healing fantasy

Questions

1. Why do negative role-selves arise?
2. What factors influence role-selves?
3. How can role-selves sabotage future intimate relationships?
4. Mention what you've learned about role-selves?
5. Fill in the blank to discover your role self. Don't think about it too much, just fill it with the first thing that comes to your mind.

i.   I wish other people were more _____

ii.   Why is it so hard for people to _____

iii.   For a change, I would love someone to treat me like _____

iv.   Maybe one of these days I'll find someone who will _____

v.   I try hard to be _____

vi.   The main reason people like me is because I _____

vii.   Other people don't appreciate how much I _____

viii. I always have to be the one who _____

ix.   I've tried to be the kind of person who _____

x.   Use your answer to write two short descriptions about yourself. One about your role self and the other about your role self.

6. List the differences between the worldview of internalists and externalists.

7. Identify your approach to life, response to problems, psychological style, and relationship style.

8. Based on your answer to the previous questions would you describe yourself as an internalizer or an externalizer?

CHAPTER 6: WHAT IT'S LIKE TO BE AN INTERNALIZER

Summary

All internalizers are extremely perceptive and highly sensitive to those around them. They have a strong desire to connect with those around them.

They have strong desires but they don't like to be a bother which is why they are usually emotionally neglected.

For these ones, their role-self focuses on others and they create a peculiar healing fantasy that can change the feelings and attitudes they receive from others.

They get little or no support from others and they expect little or nothing from others because they don't want to be a bother and also because their active minds can come up with something.

In their relationships, internalizers easily get burnt out because they don't know when giving from their emotional bank is too much.

Key takeaways from this chapter

- Since they are perceptive, internalizers know when they are truly connecting with others. They have strong emotions so the effect of having emotionally immature parents affects them terribly. Loneliness is a burning sting to them.

- When they are told they have a behavioral problem, the message internalizers receive is that their nature is the problem.
- They have an innate desire for deep connections. They long to share their deepest inner experiences and feelings. They want to engage emotionally and they are hurt when they get a blank emotionless face.
- They read people to be sure they are making a connection. They believe that if they hide their feelings while helping their parents, they will win their love. They believe that love and connection come at a cost which is putting others first and treating them as more important.
- They have strong instincts for genuine emotional engagement. This is a basic instinct all mammals including humans have and need.
- Even though externalizers desire emotional comfort, they force it on others. It makes it feel like they are taking others hostage emotionally due to their outbursts and reactivity. They use their attitude to manipulate others into giving a response.
- Many emotionally immature people are externalizers which makes it difficult or almost impossible for them to calm down through genuine emotional engagement. Those who get terribly upset seem like they have a strong drive towards emotional engagement but anyone who is perceptive will see that they are panicking not connecting.
- Internalizers feel embarrassed and undeserving when they seek help or therapy. They don't expect anyone to take their feelings seriously. If they got shamed for showing sensitive emotions as

children, they may be embarrassed to show any genuine emotion as adults.

- They get by with little support. They learn from previous experiences and utilize what they learn.

- They may not have the words to express it, but they understand that they grew up emotionally lonely even though they may not know what's wrong. They have memories to show that they weren't loved or protected as children.

- They usually teach themselves to toughen up and they reject their attitude towards their feelings. They know how to detach from deep emotions or painful feelings.

- Since internalizers always look inward to find answers, they hardly term abusive situations as abusive. They take on the emotional work their parents are supposed to do due to their perceptive nature.

- Internalizers believe sacrificing themselves (which is the same as self-neglect) will make them the right candidates to love.

Lessons

- Internalizers are very sensitive. Research shows they may have been born with an alert nervous system.

- The ability to turn to others for comfort when stressed is a good thing.

- Unlike internalizers, externalizers demand attention from others by manipulating or guilt-tripping them. People feel they have to help them or respond to them because they have no other choice.

- All humans need emotional connection because it is a life saver. It might be the only thing that gets you through tough times or a rough day.
- We all need a deep sense of connection to feel safe and the beauty in it is that there's nothing wrong with it.
- Internalizers will always attract needy people due to their nature.

Goals

- To understand internalizers
- To know if you're an internalizer
- To determine how much of an internalizer you are
- To determine the importance of emotional connection
- To distinguish between an internalizer and an externalizer's need and manner of the search for emotional connection

Action plans

- Understanding internalizers
- Observing yourself to know if you're an internalizer
- Understanding the traits of internalizers
- Understanding the importance of emotional connection
- Distinguishing between an internalizer and externalizer's need for emotional connection and making the right adjustments.

Questions

1. Do you think internalizers are highly sensitive? If yes, is it a good thing?

2. Have you ever tried to calm an externalizer down? How did it feel? Narrate your experience.

3. Do you think it's easy to neglect internalizers? Explain the reason behind your answer.

4. Why are internalizers overly independent?

CHAPTER 7: BREAKING DOWN AND AWAKENING

Summary

Your true self wants to be known, wants to grow, and wants to show who it really is while seeking your expansion. It also wants you to accept it.

No matter how well we play our self-roles and live out our healing fantasies, the true self will always find a way to display itself.

Some people have learned to hide their true selves no matter how much it tries to come to the fore. The downside to this is that they may begin to exhibit some psychological symptoms.

To say that facing and expressing your true self can be discombobulating wouldn't be an exaggeration. At first, it can feel like you're going to break down as panic, depression, anger and other intense emotions begin to find their way to the surface. Take this as a sign of an emotional awakening to healthy values and improved self-care.

As long as you decide to process your childhood emotional issues, you'll see how strong you are. This will give you the boost you need to confidently be true to yourself and live your true life.

Emotional turmoil is a sign that it's getting difficult to remain emotionally unconscious and we are about to find our true selves that lie beneath our healing fantasies.

Key takeaways from this chapter

- The true self is who we really are deep within. It is true because it isn't affected by pressures or other external factors.

- The true self is what directs individuals to the right functioning and optimal energy. It helps to focus on solutions, not problems.

- Children can live from their true selves if parents or caregivers help them see that they need to do so. When they are shamed or criticized, they pretend to be someone else that the parents want, pushing their true selves deeper within.

- A breakdown happens when the pain of healing fantasies and living in role selves is more than any potential benefits.

- When the true self is tired of role-playing, the individual usually gets the wake-up call by experiencing unexpected emotions or emotional signs.

- Internalists don't take care of themselves because they believe they are supposed to fix everything so they neglect their health, rest, and ignore the signs of pain and fatigue.

- Problems in relationships are our opportunities to wake up from our role selves.

- It's an illusion to believe that our parents are wiser and more knowledgeable because they are our parents. We need to wake up from it.

- You need to know your strengths and articulate it. This will give you self-validation and boost your esteem and your part in this world.

- The best way to wake up from repeating the past is to go through the mental and emotional pain from childhood.

Lessons

- The true self is not a new concept. It goes as far back as ancient times when people began to discover the concept of the soul. It tells us who a person truly is. It is the source of intuition, gut feeling, and the right perception of other people.

- Your true self wants you to live in and from reality.

- If you're experiencing a breakdown, ask yourself what exactly is breaking down.

- When you give up the healing fantasy of how you expect to find love, you will begin to face the unwanted feelings about the people who are close to you.

- If you continue to push down your real feelings for too long, they may come out in unexpected ways that will force you to stop and find out what's wrong.

- One emotion that expresses individuality is anger. It is what emotionally immature parents lash out at their children the most.

- Intimate relationships arouse emotions so they activate unresolved emotional issues. We project issues from our parents on our partners which will lead to anger because it reminds us of issues from the past as well as what is currently happening in a relationship.

- It feels better to stay naïve about the weakness of our parents than to see them objectively.

- What happened to you isn't as important as processing what happened to you.

Goals

- To understand what the true self is all about
- To know your true self
- To know the signs of your true self calling out to you
- To know what is breaking down
- To release yourself from a defeating self role
- To wake up to what you truly feel
- To explore whether you have hidden feelings
- To wake up through relationship breakdowns
- To wake up from idealizing others
- To wake up to your strength and a new set of values
- To be free from childhood issues

Action Plans

- Understanding the true self and differentiating it from the role self
- Knowing your true self
- Interpreting the signs that your true self sends to you
- Understand what is breaking down
- Releasing yourself from a defeating self role
- Waking up to your feelings
- Waking up from idealizing others
- Acting from your strength and your new set of values
- To be childhood injury and trauma-free

Questions

1. Get a piece of paper; fold it lengthwise from the middle so it allows you to see both half sides at once. On one side, write 'my true self.' On the other side, write 'my role self'. On the side of your true self, honestly write about who you were before you wanted to become someone else. What made you feel good? What did you enjoy? Who were your favorite people and why?

2. What do you do for people to love, accept and admire you? What do you tell yourself to do, so people will think you're a good person? What do you do but you don't like it? What takes up your time but is boring to you? What perspective do you want others to have about you? What parts about yourself do you try to hide from others?

3. Compare your answers to question 1 and question 2. Are you living from your true self or from your self-role?

4. Can anger, rage, anxiety, depression, and other similar emotions be a good thing? Explain the reasons for your answer?

5. Why are people comfortable playing role-selves even as adults?

6. Who makes you anxious or nervous and why? How does your self-role show when you're around the person? Do you think it's time for the self-role to go? Are you ready to see yourself differently?

7. Why do you feel guilty or shame for feelings that you think are unacceptable?

8. When you feel anxious or depressed, ask yourself if you're harboring hidden feelings. Think about other times you felt that

way. Was it the same thing that fuelled that thought? Write out everything about this thought.

9. How can anger be a good emotion?

CHAPTER 8: HOW TO AVOID GETTING EMOTIONALLY HOOKED BY AN EMOTIONALLY IMMATURE PARENT

Summary

Just as babies were born to be dependent, every child is meant to be dependent on parents. This phenomenon includes seeking their attention, love, and affection.

Adopting the maturity awareness approach is a great way to manage an emotionally immature parent or anyone who reminds you or acts like one.

You need to first relate with your parents objectively rather than build a relationship with them.

Before you progress with building a relationship with your parents, identify the level of maturity of your parents.

Key takeaways from this chapter

- To gain emotional freedom, you must first determine if both or either of your parents is emotionally immature.
- To handle a parent who is emotionally immature (or both parents as the case may be), there are approaches to gain your freedom and gain emotional immaturity. They are detached observation, maturity awareness, and stepping away from your old role self.

Detached observation

- You need to act from your true nature, not the self-role that pleases your parents. Emotionally immature parents encourage enmeshment instead of individual identity. Enmeshment is when your parents don't respect boundaries by getting too involved in your issues and casting their own unresolved issues on you.
- In an enmeshed family, when you have issues with someone, you talk about the issues to someone else instead of the person you're having issues with.

Becoming observational

- When you're observational, you'll find out you're more centered, logical, and calm when relating with an emotionally immature person.
- Always get into an observational and detached position when you want to relate with an emotionally immature person.
- While becoming observational, if you notice that you're getting emotional, it means you're back into healing fantasy mode. There's an unpleasant feeling that makes you feel like you're weak and needy, which is a sign that you're emotional and need to get back into the observation mode.
- Relatedness and relationship are different. In relatedness, there's communication with no goal of a satisfying emotional exchange while a relationship involves openness, vulnerability, and emotional reciprocity.

Maturity awareness

- Maturity awareness involves determining the maturity level of the person you're relating with.
- Your interaction with your parents should be solely objective (logical, not emotional) then you can progress to the three steps of maturity awareness which are

i.   Expressing yourself and letting go

ii.   Don't focus on the relationship but on the outcome

iii.   Managing interaction not emotional engagement

Expressing and letting go

- Express yourself calmly without judging the other person. Don't try to influence the outcome.

Focusing on the outcome, not the relationship

- The first thing you need to determine is the goal of the interaction. Is it for the other person to see your pain, to understand you, to hurt the person, to apologize, or to make amends? If your goal is for your parents to change, then stop and come up with another goal. You need to identify the specific outcome you want from your interaction.
- Don't engage emotionally immature people, rather, set goals to manage interaction, give a timeframe to the interaction and make sure your mind is active. This might mean that you redirect conversations when it's veering off the logical and unemotional route it is meant to go.

- As a child grows to become an individual, emotionally immature parents do things that force the child into an enmeshed pattern. If the child doesn't adapt to this pattern, parents begin to relate with them in a genuine respectful way. Sometimes, this can make you vulnerable and you get sucked into your healing fantasy, so you have to stay observant and relate with them objectively as a separate adult.

Lessons

- Emotionally immature parents are focused on their own healing fantasy and they expect their children to correct their childhood pain.
- Emotionally immature parents promote emotional enmeshment over individual identity.
- When you keep yourself in a neutral position while observing your parents, you can't be ensnared emotionally or hurt by the other person's behavior.
- Staying observational is an active process.
- It's better to opt for relatedness and keep relationships with people who can reciprocate a relationship.
- Maturity awareness is about pegging the emotional maturity/immaturity of the person you're relating with so their responses become more predictable.
- When expressing and letting go, remember that you can't force people to change, understand or empathize.

- If you're dealing with an empathetic person, it's okay to address emotional issues in a relationship.
- When dealing with emotionally immature parents, focus on the desired outcome for your interaction so you can stay observant and objective no matter what they do to you.
- Your parents will always be available to you to the same level at which you need them.

Goals

- To learn how to relate with your parents
- To protect your emotions
- To change the fantasy that a parent will change
- To forge a new relationship
- To become observational
- To step out of an old role-self
- To keep a grip on your thoughts and feelings

Action plan

- Staying observant when relating with your parents
- Protecting your emotions
- Changing your fantasy about your parents
- Forging a new relationship
- Becoming observational
- Stepping out of your old role self
- Getting a grip on your emotions and feelings

Questions

1. What are the beliefs about your parents that you had as a child? Is it that they know what's best for you or they love you no matter what or they will always be there for you or they would never hurt you? Mention them.

2. Do you still believe your responses to the previous question and why?

3. Is there someone who makes you anxious and nervous? What can you do to become observational when relating with such a person? Would you hold your breath or act like a scientist? Would you tell yourself to detach? Explain what you can do.

CHAPTER 9: HOW IT FEELS TO LIVE FREE OF ROLES AND FANTASIES

Summary

Children of emotionally immature parents usually have a role self that wants to please their parents even if it means rejecting themselves, their thoughts, and feelings.

If you have learned to reject yourself due to the deep inner critical voice that wants you to be perfect, it is possible to reclaim your true self and let go of the inhibitions from others.

Accept yourself. This means that you claim your freedom, be who you are, and consider yourself (not neglect yourself) when taking action or making decisions. If you need to grieve over all you've lost (due to your kind of parents), take the time to do so.

You also need to be self-compassionate and invest in self-care. This means you need to stop giving more than normal or overextending yourself when it isn't necessary. You don't have to give too much empathy to others. When you begin to consider yourself, you'll find out that your parents will respect your boundaries as you're no longer needy for their acceptance and love, while you're honest with your relationship with them without expecting them to change.

Key takeaways from this chapter

- Growing up with an emotionally immature parent means you may have a fear of individuality because this is a threat to such a parent.

- Emotionally immature parents try to manage their anxieties by training their children on how to think, feel, respond and live. Internalizers turn this into a way of life and see that their inner experiences have no authenticity.

- Internalized children stifle enthusiasm, spontaneity, uninhabited affection, anger, pain, loss, grief, and what they want to say or feel. They would rather embrace obedience to authorities, self-doubt, physical illness or injuries that put them at the mercy of their parents, stereotyped gender roles, guilt and shame over imperfections, willingness to listen to parents complain, and liking what their parents liked.

- Internalized children accept many self-defeating things to get on with life. It includes giving consideration to what others want first, not asking for help, not wanting anything for yourself, and not speaking up for yourself.

- Parent-voice internalization is how parents train their children to go against their instinct. This voice is a non-stop inner commentary that lives within. The voice sounds like your voice. The voice can make you feel bad and spread shame and guilt within you so you need to interrupt this voice.

- You need to allow all your emotions and thoughts without allowing guilt or shame to stifle you.

- If you need to suspend contact with your parents, then do this. It may bring up guilt and self-doubt but you need to remember that it's for your good. This will help your parents to respect boundaries with you.

- You don't need to have a relationship with your parents to detangle yourself from their influence. Some people have lost their parents yet they aren't free from their influence.

- To set limits and boundaries, control how involved you are with your parents so you can spend your energy and emotions on profitable relationships. It doesn't matter if they protest; remember that it's you first!

- The two basic building blocks of strong individuality include self-sympathy and knowing your feelings. Self-compassion helps you to set boundaries so you don't give excessively.

- Practicing self-compassion will come with tears and grief; don't hinder it, just let it flow.

- When you express yourself with emotionally immature people, you're carrying out self-affirmation and showing that you're an individual with thoughts and feelings.

Lessons

- Growing up with emotionally immature parents means
  - ➢ Individuality is discouraged
  - ➢ Individual preferences and needs are not allowed
  - ➢ Always doing what your internalized parental voice wants you to do

- Internalizers see their feelings as unimportant at their peak and shameful at their worst but they can adopt a mindset change when they become aware that their mindset is distorted.

- Suppressing your inner experience is a sign of living with emotionally immature parents.

- Allowing your inner feelings and thoughts to flow naturally without any inhibitions or worry strengthens you and it brings relief.

- Accepting the truth about your thoughts and feelings isn't wrong. It only means you're human, mature, and whole.

- Some parents may never understand that their attitude is problematic.

- Pay attention to subtle energy drains.

- Practicing self-care requires self-compassion. When you practice self-compassion, you'll feel refreshed and you'll heal from within. It might seem odd initially, but you'll find out how helpful it is as you practice it continually.

- Taking action for yourself or asking for help when necessary is an antidote to the feeling of helplessness that internalizers face.

- Drop the notion that your parents would understand you if they loved you. You're an adult and you don't need their understanding.

- You may not have an ideal relationship with your parents but you can make interaction with them satisfying for you.

- Do you really need your parents or do they want you to need them? You need to answer this question honestly and objectively to progress.

Goals

- To know how freedom from role-playing feels.
- To get over emotional loneliness
- To recognize your internalized parental voice
- To be free to be imperfect and human
- To allow your feelings and thoughts
- To be free to withhold or restrict all forms of contact with your parents
- To be free to take action for yourself
- To gain the freedom to express yourself
- To gain the freedom to approach old relationships in new ways
- To be free from wanting something from your parents

Action plans

- Freedom from role playing
- Gaining emotional stability
- Identifying your parental voice
- Freedom to be imperfect and human
- Expressing your feelings and tho0.ughts
- Freedom to withhold contact with your parents
- Stepping out of the neediness of your parents
- New approaches to old relationships

Questions

1. Is there one person you don't like who takes up your energy gradually? How should you relate to such a person? Will setting boundaries help?

2. Why is it important to prevent your parent-voice from controlling you?

3. Why is it important to feel deep emotion?

4. Is there any good thing about tears and grief?

5. Why is healthy empathy important?

6. What can you do to make interaction with your parents more satisfying for you? Would it be to embrace your thoughts, avoid them, speak up politely, or stay away? Mention what you can do.

CHAPTER 10: HOW TO IDENTIFY EMOTIONALLY MATURE PEOPLE

Summary

There are better ways to relate with people that will yield the desired relationship you need. With your newfound observational skills, find the right people to connect with instead of falling back into old patterns.

Key takeaways from this chapter

Adult children of emotionally immature parents don't easily believe that relationships can make their life better. They believe rewarding relationships aren't real because they fear that if others know who they truly are, they wouldn't be interested in them.

Emotionally mature people

- Are realistic, consistent, flexible, and reliable.
- Accept reality on its terms and make the best of it.
- Are reasonable because they can feel and think at the same time. They can see different perspectives in any situation.
- Can be objective so they don't take everything personally. They understand that people can make mistakes and a mistake isn't strong enough to cause an indelible mark on you or your future.
- They are respectful and reciprocal, and they understand boundaries. They build connections with others not intrude on people's lives or take others for granted.

- They don't take advantage of others, rather they give back.
- They don't react or get angry unjustifiably because they are even-tempered.
- They have a secure sense of self, they are willing to listen to you and understand your perspective.
- They will tell you the truth because it is the basis to trust.
- They don't mind making amends when they realize they are wrong. They can apologize.
- They make you feel safe due to their empathy
- They identify you as an individual. They can see and understand you.
- They like to comfort and be comforted
- They can reflect on their behavior and make changes where necessary
- They can be playful and fun to be with. They laugh easily. It's wonderful to be around them.

When you meet someone online use the same criteria you used for emotionally mature people for them. Be observant of how they make you feel, their boundaries, and how they speak. Do they make you feel pressured? Do they talk about themselves all along? Do they think about what you're saying or do they gloss over it? Are they easy to be with? Be sure about them before committing yourself to them. There's no need to rush.

Lessons

- Familiarity means safety. We tend to be drawn to people who remind us and take us back to old patterns.
- Personal writing lets you know an individual, how they think, their perspective, their focus, and their sensitivity to others.

Goals

- To recognize emotionally mature people
- To identify what to look out for in relationships
- To identify realistic and reliable people
- To identify respectful and reciprocal people
- To be responsive
- To develop new relationship habits
- To explore new ways of being in a relationship

Action plan

- Know what to expect in new relationships
- Know those who are emotionally mature
- Identify people who are realistic, respectful, reciprocal, reliable, and responsive
- Develop new relationship habits

Questions

1. Your friend who is growing out of his role self wants to get into a relationship. Tell him the characteristics of the kind of people that he needs.

2. What mindset should you have when you're going into a relationship?

Made in the USA
Monee, IL
09 November 2022

17380755R00033

Something You Need to Know...

Sometimes we want to forget what happened to us in the past because of the trauma and pain. This is why many people live in denial. However, that's not the way forward. You need to go back and understand your past so you can face a new future. You need to shine a light on your past to see who it has made you become and what you've lost in the process.

Once you do this, you'll see that you'll become better, mature, and whole. You'll be able to discover certain hidden facts about yourself, your family, and other family patterns that seem normal to you. At a point, the truth may be overwhelming to you but you need to ask yourself if seeking the truth and self-knowledge is more important to you than self-roles or half-truth beliefs that everyone has held dear.

When you choose the path of truth and self-knowledge, you'll experience a deeper connection with the world and yourself. Everything in the present will feel real; you'll feel alive and appreciate life. This is because you've resolved the frustration and confusion you've had about your family.

You'll see that you have an opportunity to live two lives. The first one comes with pain, frustration, and confusion from your childhood and your family. The second one is optional and it brings enlightenment that comes from true freedom. It will bring peace and tranquility to you. You can live up to your potential and be truly joyful because you're free from wishful fantasies and family roles. It's a truly incredible and unexplainable feeling!

Do you think it's worth it? Is it worth living your life twice? Would you choose enlightenment and inner peace?

I'm sure you would!